THE

Miracle
of Me

AND

My Life of Miracles

THE
Miracle
of Me
AND
My Life of Miracles

CURTIS WAYNE MCCALISTER

ISBN: 979-8-89228-177-5   (Paperback)
ISBN: 979-8-89228-235-2   (Hardcover)
ISBN: 979-8-89228-178-2   (eBook)

Printed in the United States of America

TABLE OF CONTENTS

For Mom and Dad

ACKNOWLEDGMENTS

Firstly, I would like to thank Father God for giving me life! Secondly, to my birth parents, whoever they were, for putting me up for adoption. I also wish to thank my parents for adopting and raising me, and seeing to my education and happy homelife.

I would like to thank my brother-in-law, Edward Lowder II, for his continuing faith in both myself and my book of miracles, as well as his guidance along the way. I would also like to thank Rev. Jeff Clayton for his suggestion that I keep a journal of all the miracles that I've seen, and Rev. Lyle Dykstra for listening and understanding just how important these miracles were to me and what they have done for my faith. I also wish to thank everyone who has supported me in this quest to understand the meaning of these miracles as they guide me forward!

You know, I think it's a miracle that this book has even been made, and I want to thank you from the bottom of my heart for picking it up and reading it. If it weren't for a number of people telling me that I should keep a journal of all the miracles that I've had over the years, or even write a book about them, then this would have never come to be. I had been agonizing about what to do for a long time, because I'm no Shakespeare. But if you'll bear with me, I'll try to get my miracles across as succinctly as possible.

My main purpose in writing this is to let all peoples of the world know that miracles do happen, and they happen every day to average people like you and me. Even so, I would like to take this opportunity to let you know that *I am not a prophet*. I may be a visionary, but I'm not a prophet. I do not hear voices or get messages sent to my head. I am what I am—just a man who has seen many wonderful things over the years, things that we would call miracles. Or if you prefer, ultra super science that is thousands or even millions of years ahead of our current technology. You won't believe the things I've seen! It is my hope that in reading this, you too will gain true enlightenment and have your faith raised to the stratosphere, just like mine has.

If you would like to know what it is that really puzzles me about all of the miracles that have happened to me, it's this: *why* on earth would Father God *ever* choose a sinner like me to give miracles to in the first place? Who knows? After all, we "lowly" humans can't even begin to outthink or outguess Father God. Perhaps it's just the luck of the draw, or maybe

He has some plan in store for me. I can't say for sure, but what I can say is that because of all the miracles I've had, my faith is quite probably higher than that of the Pope. And I highly doubt that the Pope has seen very many true miracles! You know, I take that back. I am sure that he has at least seen that picture of the Virgin Mary that's crying tears of blood, so my humble apologies to the great Pontiff. Even though I am not Roman Catholic, I *really* like Pope Francis!

At this point, I would also like to add that I do not believe the coronavirus is a plague sent from Father God. If anything, I think it could possibly be a test of humanity's resolve. I do not know for sure, but I do pray for everyone's health and safety during this troubling time.

Here I would like to address all the planetary scientists at NASA. When the New Horizons spacecraft flew by Pluto, don't you think there was a higher power at work to produce that heart-shaped feature? I mean, think about it. That heart could have been on the back-side of Pluto, or on any side, and yet, it was right in front where the cameras could see it! I personally believe that Father God had a lot to do with that. He wanted us to see that heart, as if to say, "Here's Pluto in all its glory! Don't forget about it!"

CHAPTER 1

Birth and Growing Up

Even though I don't live there, this is the only home I will ever know!

I'm sure everyone has heard the old adage that says, "All life is a miracle." It's true, you know. We, as flesh and blood human beings, would like to think that we can create life just by having babies. Nothing could be further from the truth! We can only create the body that will contain the baby. It is Father God who provides the spark of life: the soul. But this is not just mere conjecture on my part. You see, without a soul, there can be no life. So for those of you who have had babies that were stillborn, and excluding any physical difficulties, you did nothing wrong! It's just that at that time, there were no souls available; that's what I believe, and I will not debate any other theosophies!

As for myself, I was born on January 20, 1958, at 2:00 p.m. at Saint Luke's Hospital in downtown Kansas City, Missouri. To tell you the truth, I'm *very* glad that I was born, because I could have just as easily been aborted or thrown into the river, or even left in a trash dumpster! Unfortunately, I do not know the circumstances surrounding my birth parents, but I will be forever grateful to them, and to Father God, for having the decency of putting me up for adoption!

As it happened, there was a foundling home, or orphanage, next to the hospital, so I was placed there. Luckily, I wasn't there for very long, only about four weeks. That is when Clarence and Mary McCalister stepped in and decided that they wanted to adopt a baby, and that baby was me!

At that time, they were in their early forties, but the rules and regulations concerning adoption were fairly lax back then, so they had no problems with the adoption process. Dad even showed me the receipt and said, "It only cost $150.00 to get you out of hock." Ha, ha. Just try adopting a baby when you're in your forties! I'm sure nowadays the authorities would laugh in your face. Anyway, being unable to have children of their own, they showered me with a lot of love and attention and raised me as their own. Included in this package deal were a lot of aunts, uncles, cousins, and one grandmother, all of whom I loved very dearly! They also gave me many Christmas presents and a cake on my birthday, though they said that since my birthday was so close to Christmas, I wouldn't get any extra presents. I know you might think that must have been quite a bummer, but I didn't mind too much, I was just really happy to get a cake! And that's all I've wanted ever since! I'm very easy to deal with, you see.

We lived in a house that was north of the Missouri River at 4701 NE 46th Street, so we were close to just about everything the city had to offer. Dad had a job as a mechanic at Kansas City Power and Light's Hawthorne Power Station, while Mom had a job at Luce-Packwood Luggage Company that was located a block east of the big Montgomery Ward store on Belmont. Although, after they adopted me, she quit working in order to raise me.

Life was pretty ordinary for me while I was growing up in the 1960's. As a matter of fact, I think I was very privileged and blessed to have grown up in such a wonderful time! After all, I got to see the Beatles on the Ed Sullivan Show, NASA's first space missions, the moon landing, the advent of computers, newer car models, the end of segregation, newer and more fantastic TV shows and movies, low gas prices, low grocery prices, and so much more! Remember the Fuller Brush man going door to door? Boy, I sure do! I know a lot of people think that the 1960s were a bad decade fraught with assassinations, war, riots, astronaut deaths, and other stuff. All that may be true, but I don't care what they say! I still believe it was a *great* time to be alive! *God, how I miss the 60s!*

Actually, there were two events during this time that really stand out in my memory. The first happened when I was three years old. Yes, I can actually remember being three years old! Dad was in the hospital and had an operation on his back. I can still remember standing at the front screen door of our house and watched as an ambulance bearing Dad pulled into our driveway. The attendants then took out a gurney from the back and wheeled Dad into the bedroom and placed him in his bed. At that time, I still had a baby crib to sleep in, and mom put me in it before the men came in. I just stood there looking at Dad, watching him.

The second memory was when mom and I went downtown by bus to do some shopping at Macy's and the Jones store. When we were done, we went into what I later discovered was a restaurant called Horn and Hardart. I'm sure some of you might remember them! It was called an Automat. Inside, all of the walls were brown. One wall was nothing but a bank of small doors with windows, kind of like a mail slot, but these contained food. So, you go in, get a handful of change from the change machine, and put money in the slots next to where the food is. Money in, you open the door and retrieve your meal! You had to put money in to get everything: main dish, sides, salads, and dessert. I thought this was *the* greatest thing I had ever seen in my life up to then. It was unbelievable!

Anyway, sorry for digressing a bit. My second miracle, if you can call it that, happened when I was only six years old. It was a cold winter's night, and I was freezing. The furnace was set to around seventy-two to seventy-three degrees, I think; might have been higher or lower. I was in a single bed with a sheet, a blanket, a bedspread, and a blanket on top. Well, I was still cold so I got out of bed and told mom. She immediately put a quilt on my bed and ushered me back into it.

Now, you would think that would be the end of it, right? Nope. I was still cold, probably because back then, I didn't have very much body fat. I was really thin. For some unknown reason, I have always been very cold-blooded. Even today, my temperature stays in the low to mid-nineties. Then, to my good fortune, I had an epiphany. Dad had an air duct at the foot of his bed. Only about a quarter of it stuck out enough to see, the rest was under his bed. Well, I thought to myself, if that's where the warm air is, then that's where I needed to be! So I got out of bed and crawled under Dad's. The first couple of times, I didn't take a pillow or a blanket with me. But, after that, I started taking both. And, boy, did I sleep well! Back then, our furnace was one of those big old 125,000 BTU models, and it *really* put out the heat!! If I got too warm, no problem, I just moved a little further away.

I believe it was sometime after that when my parents took me to the Clay County Mental Health Department to have my IQ checked. I guess they thought a child of only six years wouldn't be able to put two and two together enough to have such a thought, who can say? I don't know, maybe an angel spoke to me, or maybe I just watched Dad put on his shoes enough times while sitting in his chair that was against the wall in front of the air duct. It took him a while because of his brace. You see, his operation, even though successful, had left his right foot completely numb. He had to wear a brace so his foot wouldn't turn in. Anyway, I got so used to crawling under his bed and getting warm, I continued doing that until I was about eleven years old. That's when I grew too big to get under there anymore. However, even if I couldn't go under the bed, there were still plenty of air ducts throughout the house where I could still lay. The living room was my primary place, but under the kitchen table also sufficed. Even to this day, though I am a man of sixty-three years and it's a little embarrassing to admit, I still like to sleep by the air ducts in the winter. Also, a year earlier, I had somehow managed—don't ask me how—to discover that there was no Santa Claus. I know that's an awfully young age to find that out, but perhaps my IQ was indeed fairly high. You see, whether or not it was scientifically proven that I was a genius, I am still quite an eccentric individual!

At this point, before we get to the major miracles that have happened to me over the years, I want to let you know that I am Presbyterian by faith and that I have never considered myself to be very religious, and I'm not a righteous individual either. Church was just something we did every Sunday when I was growing up. Sure, I was in choir, Sunday school, and I went to camp. I participated in all the activities of my age group, made friends, and went to regular school with most of them.

Don't get me wrong, I really liked our ministers and the services, but sometimes I didn't quite understand what was being said. One time, back in the 60s, our minister was on television and spoke about something or other. I can't remember what it was about, but I was shocked and thought it was being broadcast live! It wasn't, but how was I to know that? My Dad told me to call the minister to let him know I saw him. I didn't think it was possible, because being a little kid, I thought for sure he was still at the TV station! Imagine my surprise when he answered the phone! This was all back during the time that Jack Lalane was on TV doing exercises early each morning and getting the audience at home to join in, which I did from time to time. As I got older, I became an Elder in the Church, and at one point back in 1998, I actually got up in front of everyone and preached a sermon. I think I just wanted to get the Minister's point of view, and see what the service looked like. Believe it or not, I still have that sermon. I found it just the other day!

CHAPTER 2

The Temple in the Sky

A close facsimile

At this point, I would like to begin the really big miracles, and the first one is a full-blown *wowza!* It happened when I was thirteen years old. My mom, dad, and I were coming back from doing some business in Liberty, Missouri, and I was in the back seat of Dad's Plymouth Fury 3. We were rounding the Glenaire curve on I-35 when I happened to look out of my window at the western sky. Perhaps I was made to look. What I saw was *truly* astonishing! I didn't think it possible, but there it was, a Greek-style temple—*completely made out of clouds*—floating in the sky! It had a hipped roof, had ten columns on its long axis, two on either side of the massive front doors, and two steps in front. It was flat on the bottom, and just floated along like it belonged there!

My first thought was that this *had* to be the Temple of Solomon! My second thought was that it was too bad I didn't have a camera in my hand! I had never seen a picture of what the real Temple of Solomon looked like, but I thanked Father God for allowing me to see this miraculous sight! Because He really loved the Temple of Solomon so much, I believe that *this* is how He travels around to check on the things He's made. You see, Father God tends to put things in a perspective that we "lowly" humans can understand. After all, He's billions of years ahead of us in technology! Who do you think first invented the arts, music, trees, landscapes, grass, animals, mechanical technologies, and us? The alternative to this way of thinking would be that maybe the Greek gods are actually real! But *that* would be extremely hard to swallow. My belief, however, is *firmly* stated above! To this day I still look at the clouds, hoping that I might get to see it again. However, I'm afraid that if I do, there is a chance that Father God might decide to take me along with him.

CHAPTER 3

The Value of Three

This chapter nearly didn't get included in this book. It took a while for me to remember it, and it happened well before the things I now know. This miracle occurred around the time of my Mom's passing in December of 1994, when I was dating the friend of a friend of my wife's, and this was before I ever met my wife! My wife's friend was the roommate of my girlfriend. You can't make this stuff up folks! Anyway, my girlfriend was a dialysis nurse at North Kansas City Hospital. A childhood friend of mine did the maintenance on the various IV machines, and he asked me if I would be willing to date this gal. I said I would, and I'm sure glad I did!

As I said before, my Mom was in the hospital at that time. She had a bad heart, and needed oxygen at night due to sleep apnea. Two days before she passed, she underwent a colonoscopy. I heard that the walls of her intestine had ruptured in several places due to excessive pressure. (Just so you know, Dad never pressed charges against the doctor or the hospital.) Well, I guess the pain was *so* bad that on the second night, she left the oxygen off and passed in her sleep. I called my girlfriend and she came over as quickly as she could. I was in shock for several days and wouldn't set foot in Mom's bedroom! On her deathbed, Mom told me that I was a genius.

But there was one thing my girlfriend neglected to mention, and that was the fact that both her Father *and* her roommate's Father were dying of cancer at the same exact time. One week after my Mom passed, my girlfriend's father passed, and a week after that, her roommate's father passed. Trust me when I tell you that three funerals in such a short length of time can be quite unnerving!

We all know how much Father God loves the number three, and so many things in this world happen in threes. You see, the three of us were put together purposefully in order to comfort each other. It is true that Father God does work in mysterious ways, and this was one of those times when people needed to be brought together to serve a common purpose. Grief, comfort, and compassion work hand in hand with each other. So it's okay to grieve for your loved one. It's a natural process that helps us heal inside. But I know that the ones who pass would rather we celebrate their life and be happy for them. I was in too much shock to grieve for my Mom, but I did cry when my Dad passed. However, I did not cry when my wife died. It wasn't that I didn't care about her, it was just that I knew a lot more than I did at the time Mom passed. Believe me, knowing what I now know about the other side really helps with grief.

Even so, I will be forever grateful to these two wonderful people for their strength, courage, and kindness during this sad time. LeAnne, and Bea: *thank you, from the bottom of my heart!* If it weren't for you, I really don't know how I would have coped with Mom's passing. After all, this was a first for me as I've never had to deal, both emotionally and physically, with the death of a close family member.

Up to this point, I've only had aunts and uncles pass. As you'll learn further on, I've never been good at handling death.

At the time this occurred, I hadn't even considered that it might have been a miracle. Only after some time had passed did I truly give it credence, but then I completely forgot about it. That's why this chapter was almost never included.

The Pallet in the Air

Not an actual Grainger photo

The next big miracle is probably *the flashiest* of all and happened in 2006, when I was working at the W.W. Grainger Regional Distribution Center off 210 Highway here in Kansas City. At that time, I was working in the Customer Direct Order (CDO) Department. My job was that of stock keeper/order filler. But before I get too far into this, allow me to tell you about the inside layout of the warehouse. The building itself is 1.4 *million* square feet of storage space. It's really *huge!* It's divided into nine equal sections, the first three being on the southern side of the building and included the Receiving Department. The next three were in the middle, which included the Shipping Department to the west, and the last three were on the northern side of the building. There is a wide main aisle separating Sections 1, 4, and 7 from 2, 5, and 8, and another one separating Sections 2, 5, and 8 from 3, 6, and 9. My department was in front of the Receiving Department in Section 2.

I was driving a Raymond forklift at that time and had picked up an order that required me to go over to Section 3, which had a series of picking aisles and storage racks. Fortunately, the order I had told me to go straight down the aisle I was in to meet its counterpart in Section 3. When I got to the main cross aisle, that's when I saw it. Right in front of me was what looked like one of Grainger's disposable 36-inch x 42-inch pallets literally *hanging* in the air! It was about fifteen feet away and seemed to be hanging at the height of the fifth level racks, *and* it was also *see-through.* It was like smoke, I could see things on the other side. Not only that, it also appeared to have a lightning bolt surrounding it! The bolt seemed to be pulsating in and out, in and out, constantly.

I immediately looked around to see if anyone else had seen this marvelous thing. There was not a soul in sight, not even in receiving. The warehouse appeared to be totally deserted! Then, I put my hand up in front of my eyes to see if the image was being sent to my brain, or if it was really there. The image was blocked and when I took my hand down, the image was still there. After that, I got down from my forklift and got on my knees, thanking and praising Father God for allowing me to see this wondrous sight.

After a while, though, I kind of sensed that this pallet wanted me to follow it, so I hopped back on my lift and proceeded down the aisle. The pallet stayed in front of me at its same height and distance as we continued on. We went past the first small cross aisle, and came to the second one. Here, I had to turn left and go around the corner to the next aisle over. It was then that the pallet vanished, and much to my surprise, in front of me at the height of level five was a *real* pallet just barely hanging onto the rack by its wooden lip! Since I was the Safety Representative for our department, I immediately got on the radio and called for someone to come out there with a manned box to get it down before it fell on some unsuspecting order filler! That thing could have killed someone. Thank Father God, it did not!

After I'd had some time to ponder this object, it occurred to me what this thing actually was. It was a holographic image with no visible means of transmission. But no one on Earth has this kind of technology! We can't as yet beam images from one place to another, or through solid matter. It also occurred to me that no one else was around because Father God sent signals to everyone's scanner guns to get them out of the way. I was the only one allowed to see the image! Wow! You know, I've also wondered if perhaps this was how Moses had seen the burning bush, with the lightning bolt surrounding it. Ancient people would definitely have said that it looked like it was on fire, but was not being consumed.

Within the past five years, I actually wrote a letter to the personnel manager at Grainger and told them about this, but they never replied. Oh, I also told a friend who I used to work with at Grainger; we both go to the same church! She couldn't believe it either!

CHAPTER 5

The Girl

Actual Barnes and Noble photo

The next miracle happened in 2014 during the week after Christmas. I decided to go to the Barnes and Noble Booksellers in Zona Rosa, which is a shopping district in Parkville, Missouri. I'm a big fan of Japanese manga and anime, so I wanted to see if there were any new books in my current series. When I rode the escalator up to the second floor, I began to hear a loud voice coming from a few aisles over. It was a girl's voice, and she was being rather obnoxious, even while talking to other people. Purposely or not, I couldn't tell. I wondered what was up, so I approached the aisle. Then a young girl with dark hair of about fifteen or sixteen years of age came around the corner. She was bundled up in a heavy winter coat, a hat, earmuffs, and a scarf. With the earmuffs on, it's no wonder she couldn't hear very well, and would explain her loud voice. Even so, I was still a little curious why she hadn't taken any of her clothing off, because the store was fairly warm. Anyway, I looked through the shelves, found a book to read then checked to see if any chairs were available to sit in. They were all taken, so I decided to just sit on the floor and read a little of the book I'd found. That's when this girl did the oddest thing. For some reason that I was completely unaware of, this young girl suddenly decided that she would sit next to me! I was flabbergasted! Why would she do this? When I said next to me, I mean she was right up against me, with no spaces. I, for one, didn't think it was appropriate. It was like she knew me or something, but I didn't know her. At least I didn't think I did. Do you think a young girl of that age would just sit right next to a fifty- six-year-old man whom she didn't even know? I don't think so!

I hear you asking yourself, "So, where's the miracle in all of this?" The miracle, my friends, is this: after much postulating, I have concluded that she had to be someone close to me, like either my Mom—who, if you remember, passed away back in 1994, or my Aunt Betty who passed in 2000. That has to be the answer! If this is true, it would explain why she didn't remove any of her clothing; she didn't want to be recognized. We did speak briefly, and she even sounded like mom would at that age! Even so, I'll let you decide.

CHAPTER 6

Dad

Immanuel Presbyterian Church

My next miracle took place in late 2015 or early 2016, and it was by far the greatest to me, personally. It happened at church, believe it or not, during a regular service. But before I get too far into it, let me tell you a little bit more about my father. Dad was born in northern Texas in 1914. He served in the U.S. Army during the Second World War, achieving the rank of Corporal Technician. He married Mom just before he enlisted, and passed away in 2007 in Hill City, Kansas, at the age of 92. There is a reason I'm telling you this here, which will become clear momentarily.

Anyway, I had to go to the bathroom during the minister's sermon. No laughing! After I got my business done and was washing my hands, I heard the door open, and then a voice said, "Oh, so that's what you look like now! I almost didn't recognize you without hair!"

I turned around and there stood a young man of 18 or 19 years of age, with white hair, navy blue pants, and a light blue dress shirt. I was about to say, "Do I know you?" but was just too dumbfounded to reply. As I was pondering this young man, I happened to see his reflection in the mirror. It seemed very bright around his head, and I even thought to myself, *Why is it so bright up there?*

When I finished, I said goodbye and returned to my seat in the sanctuary. It was only then that I started putting two and two together. I thought his attire looked very familiar, but I think it was the hair that clinched it for me. Just then, a shock ran through my body, and I almost fainted. Oh my God! That was Dad! And just like the girl in the previous chapter, he was totally corporeal. He was a solid person and not a ghost. But he was wearing the same clothes he was buried in. Not only that, Dad told me some years ago that he had white hair before he turned twenty-one. It was also the way he spoke to me—like he knew me!

I have never seen any pictures of Dad as a young man before, but there was a picture of him taken in 1917, when he was three years old, that I have seen. I also thought that he didn't sound or even look like himself. I guess it would take a few years for his appearance to change. I did have some pictures of him when he was in the service. At that time, he was twenty-seven years old and looked like the father I knew. And as for the bright light around his head, I thought to myself, "Well, duh—halo!"

You see, during that period, I was under a lot of stress and I even remember praying for Dad to help me if he could. So I think Dad came back to reassure me, to let me know that everything will be all right. Truth be told, I felt greatly relieved after seeing him.

From what I have gathered from the two people that I've seen, once we die, we are given a new flesh and blood body that can exist in both planes of existence. Unless they are some of the elite on the other side—and by elite I mean people like Lord Jesus, the Virgin Mary, Joseph, or any of the angels— their halos can only be seen in mirrors, so you won't ordinarily see one.

I know a lot of you out there might think that Father God doesn't bring people back. In fact, I even had a Pastor at a Lutheran Church scoff at me and tell me that. But if Father God could make Adam out of clay, then He can make a body for anyone, anytime he wants to. That's what I believe. Perhaps there is a way that the dearly-departed can get permission to come back for brief visits. I've heard about it on television shows and seen it for myself, and I know a lot of you have also seen relatives come back—most are young because everyone on the other side has been made young again. Sometimes they may come back older because that's the only way you have seen them, either in real life or in a photo. My brother-in-law told me that one week after his oldest sister's funeral, he had just got out of a movie theater and was getting into his car when he heard her voice in his conscious mind telling him that she was just fine on the other side, which was very emotionally moving to him. He said he felt a sense of security in what she said. The second time he heard her voice was when he was praying in church. He said it was again in his mind, but she sounded nervous like she was being ushered away because she got caught talking to him without permission. The third time, he was at church again and during a communal prayer, he heard her voice, but couldn't make out anything clearly. He said it was like she was yelling, and then her voice faded away. He said this was the last time he heard from her. I'm sure that this sort of interpersonal communication happens more than we might like to think, and not only does it give us peace of mind, but also peace of heart as well.

By the way, have any of you ever seen or heard about a movie called *Heaven Is for Real*? If you haven't seen it, please check it out. It's amazing. There is a lot in that movie that corroborates many of the things I've seen. What's in the movie is true, and I believe it to be true!

CHAPTER 7

Skyler and Business

Business Card

The next thing to happen to me might just be more of a coincidence than a true miracle, it just depends on how you look at it. It was on a Saturday night and my stepson, Skyler, wanted to go over to Kansas with some friends of his. They loaded up their car and took off. So far, it was nothing out of the ordinary. As evening drew near, I started to get hungry and wanted a burger. Ah, but where to get it? We have both a Wendy's and a Burger King fairly close to the house. Decisions, decisions.

I decided that I wanted a big flame-grilled burger, so I went to the Burger King that was in North Kansas City, which we refer to as Northtown. Just as I was passing by the front of the store, I saw Skyler in the parking lot waving his arms at me. I pulled in and went over to him. He said their car broke down and he needed a ride back home. I was kind of dumbfounded. Wow! It crossed my mind that maybe I was directed here on purpose! Perhaps I was. Who can say for sure? This was the last thing to happen to me that could be considered a miracle—at least so far.

Since that time, I feel like Father God has been guiding me and motivating me not only to tell people about my miracles, but to also counsel them about their loved one's passing. I even started a business called "Afterlife Consulting" and even though I'm not a licensed professional, with all the miracles I've had I feel more than qualified to let people know that passing is more akin to moving away from friends and family. And it shouldn't feel any worse than if they moved to Cleveland or to Europe! You may not be able to see them or hear them, but you can be assured that they are very much alive and safe on the other side. It's not a bad thing, it's a good thing. They will become young again and will be in perfect health! Also, I have pledged to give a quarter of my fee to the family's local church or designated charity!!

I'm just starting out, so I haven't had much of an opportunity to advertise. I have business cards and a yard sign so far, plus I have visited a number of area churches. Even so, I do understand that the subject matter is not one that most people would like to talk about, ever. However, I feel that if they just knew the things I know, and seen the things I've seen, they would be at peace with the world and themselves, and their faith would also be boosted to new heights! Maybe they too will feel like they "have more faith than the Pope!"

It's kind of funny in a way, because I used to be afraid of death. When I was real little, around five or six years of age, Dad took me to the visitation of a friend of his. He was holding me and told me that I could touch the dead man's face, which I did. I think that may have unconsciously traumatized me! Ever since, the mere sight of a casket has spooked me. I couldn't look at one, much less get near one without having a panic attack! In 1977, a friend of mine from school and church was killed in a car accident, and his funeral was at our church.

When they were bringing his body inside, I hid in an adjacent hallway until they were at the front of the sanctuary. I stood there, trembling. I was nineteen years old at that time.

It took a lot of years for me to overcome my fear, but I have. I was even a pall-bearer at my father-in-law's funeral. I have also been to numerous visitations since, but now I have good news to share with the families. Their relatives are young again, and in perfect health!

Parents of young children who have passed, take heart. Your precious child or baby has been allowed to grow up on the other side! Don't be surprised to find them between the ages of eighteen and twenty-five when you get there! It's true that you can't see them or hear them, but that's just because they're in a different dimension. To put it simply, it's like there's an invisible wall between them and you. I'm sure you've all seen mimes that pretend there's a wall in front of them that can't be seen, it's like that. So technically, there's really not much difference between the two sides, you just undergo a change. When my sister-in-law was on her deathbed, she told her sister—my wife— that it was snowing in the room, even though there was no actual snow. If any of your relatives say this to you, please believe them! What they are seeing is the power of Father God which allows the soul to leave the body, and they will pass soon after.

Believe it or not, in book nine of *Monster Musume* by Japanese manga artist Okayado, there is a part in the back that he actually got right without even trying! In it, the character of Lala—who by the way is an Irish Dullahan, a spirit guide to help those who have passed away—says that "Death comes to all humans. For some, sooner, for others, later. But even when the body returns to earth, the soul be everlasting. To me, life and death be one and the same." She lives in a house with other monster girls, but can cross back and forth easily between Heaven and earth. Mr. Okayado didn't know how right he was!

I know I'm repeating myself here, but rest assured that your loved ones are very much alive and well on the other side. Believe me when I tell you that the other side is also watching us, all the time. They know when we've done something wrong to someone or to some animal. I do not know if it's like they see us on a TV screen or what, but they see us! They also hear our prayers to them, so please don't be afraid to talk to them as often as you can. I, myself, am constantly talking to Mom and Dad, to Father God and Lord Jesus, to my wife and to my other relatives. Let them know when you're hurting or troubled, or if you have any joys or celebrations to share. Just get it off your chest and be open to them! Who knows, if you ask a certain relative to help you out, you too may receive a visitation by that loved one who has passed. Perhaps you will feel like Paul as he spoke to the Jerusalem mob in Acts 22:15 when he said, "For you will be His witness to all men of what you have seen and heard!" I sincerely hope that you also have many miracles in your life. I wish you good luck. May God bless you and keep you, and may His countenance be made to shine upon you now and forevermore.

Thank you very much for reading.

In our attempts to better understand the nature of miracles or works of the Divine, this work is a short story from one man's perspective. He hopes to give us some peace and understanding about the afterlife or when we may have been entertained by angels who directed us to do something good for others in a moment of time.

These thoughts were graciously provided by Mr. Edward Lowder, a licensed professional therapist and paranormal investigator.

ABOUT THE AUTHOR

Mr. McCalister is a sixty-six-year-old gentleman who grew up in Kansas City, Missouri. He graduated from Winnetonka High School in 1976 in the top 10 percent of his class of 503. He earned a bachelor's degree from the University of Central Missouri in 1980.

He worked for W.W. Grainger from 1984 to 2009 and has had a myriad of other jobs. In 2016, he lost the use of his right arm and has mobility issues due to one leg being half an inch longer than the other.

In 1997, he married Jamie Lea Wood, also of Kansas City, but she passed away in early 2017. As of now, he lives with his stepson and a friend of the family whom he also considers a son.

His hobbies include collecting Japanese anime and manga and playing golf. He is a member of Immanuel Presbyterian Church in Kansas City and is currently trying to start a business called "Afterlife Consulting."

www.ingramcontent.com/pod-product-compliance
Lightning Source LLC
Chambersburg PA
CBHW040117150726
48005CB00013B/1756